# LET THE TREES ANSWER

# LET THE TREES ANSWER

Poems by Diane Marquart Moore

Photography by Victoria I. Sullivan
(Except as noted in list of photographs)

Copyright © 2018 Diane Marquart Moore

All rights reserved. Reproducing any part of this book for any purpose and in any format requires permission of the authors.

Cover photograph of Gebert Oak planted 1834 located at 541 Main St., New Iberia, LA

Cover design by Martin W. Romero

ISBN: 978-0-9997804-0-4

# ACKNOWLEDGMENTS

To my dear friend Karen Bourque for helping with the searching out and photographing of trees in south Louisiana; to my grandson, Joel, for using his good camera eye to help record photographs of California trees; to Darrell Bourque, always, who encourages me to persist with poetry, no matter what; to my dear friend, Mary Ann Wilson, who appreciates my efforts and who writes great endorsements; to Victoria Sullivan, who knows how to make excellent books; and to my grandson Martin for the beautiful cover design of this book.

"All our wisdom is stored in the trees."
—Santos Kalwar—

For my mother, Dorothy Greenlaw Marquart; my father Harold O. Marquart, Sr.; and my devoted friend Victoria Sullivan — lifetime tree huggers

# ALSO BY DIANE MARQUART MOORE

**POETRY**
- *Spring's Kiss*
- *Above the Prairie*
- *Sifting Red Dirt*
- *A Slow Moving Stream*
- *Street Sketches*
- *Corner of Birch Street*
- *Strand of Beads*
- *A Lonely Grandmother*
- *Between Plants and Humans*
- *Night Offices*
- *Departures*
- *In a Convent Garden*
- *Mystical Forest*
- *Everything is Blue*
- *Post Cards From Diddy Wah Diddy*
- *Alchemy*
- *Old Ridges*
- *Rising Water*
- *The Holy Present and Farda*
- *Grandma's Good War*
- *Afternoons in Oaxaca (Las Poesias)*
- *The Book of Uncommon Poetry*
- *Counterpoint*
- *Your Chin Doesn't Want to Marry*
- *Soaring*
- *More Crows*
- *Just Passing Through*
- *Moment Seized*

**YOUNG ADULTS**
- *Martin and the Last Tribe*
- *Martin Finds His Totem*
- *Flood on the Rio Teche*
- *Sophie's Sojourn in Persia*
- *Kajun Kween*
- *Martin's Quest*

**ADULT FICTION**
- *Redeemed by Blood*
- *Silence Never Betrays*
- *Chant of Death* with Isabel Anders
- *Goat Man Murder*
- *The Maine Event*

*Nothing for Free*

**CHILDREN**
*The Beast Beelzebufo*
*The Cajun Express*

**NON-FICTION**
*Porch Posts* with Janet Faulk-Gonzales
*Iran: In A Persian Market*
*Their Adventurous Will*
*Live Oak Gardens*
*Treasures of Avery Island*

# LIST OF PHOTOGRAPHS
## Photographs by Victoria Sullivan, except as noted

Hemlock: Fairbanks Circle, Sewanee, TN   3
Live Oak: Squirrel Run Golf Course, New Iberia, LA   5
Slash Pine: Celeste Dr, New Iberia, LA   9
Cottonwood: Prime Desert Woodland Preserve, Lancaster, CA, by *Joel Fontenette*   13
Cedar: Duperier Ave., New Iberia, LA   15
Joshua Tree: Rancho Vista Blvd., by *Joel Fontenette*   17
Jacaranda: next to city park, Frostproof, FL   21
Dogwood: St. Mary's Ln, Sewanee, TN   23
Red Maple: at Waffle House, New Iberia, LA   25
Mesquite: Rancho Vista Blvd., Palmdale, CA   27
Pear: Campus, University of the South, Sewanee, TN   31
Chicken Tree: Squirrel Run Golf Course, New Iberia, LA   35
Weeping Willow: Mike's Inn, New Iberia, LA   37
Crabapple: The Landscape Ranch, New Iberia, LA   41
Redbud: Chicot State Park, Ville Platte, LA   43
Bald Cypress: Squirrel Run Golf Course, New Iberia, LA   45
Crepe Myrtle: yard in New Iberia, LA   49
Catalpa: Church Point, LA, by *Karen Bourque*   51
Gebert Oak, planted 1834: 541 East Main Street, New Iberia, LA   55

# TABLE OF CONTENTS

Title    iii

Copyright    iv

Acknowledgments    v

Epigram    vi

Dedication    ix

Also By Diane Marquart Moore    xi

List Of Photographs    xiii

Table Of Contents    xv

Preface    xix

## LET THE TREES ANSWER

The Muteness Of Wooded Things    3

I See Men But They Look Like Trees Walking    5

Homecoming    9

Cottonwood    13

To A Cedar —"Gerald's Tree"    15

Joshua Tree    17

Jacaranda After Hurricane Irma, 2017    21

For Godmother Dora    23

Among The Fallen    25

The Scent Of Mesquite    27

Pearing Off    31

Oh Chicken Tree, Oh Chicken Tree    35

Weeping Willow    37

The Paradise Apple     41

Redbud     43

Bald Cypress     45

Crepe Myrtle     49

The Catawba Tree     51

Let The Trees Answer     55

**EVERYDAY JOURNAL II**

Shoe Polish Philosophy     61

Synchronicity     63

The Newspapers Foretold     65

Inner Sanctum     67

Reptilian Cold     69

Watching A Movie About Van Gogh     71

II.     73

Emergence     75

A Cardinal Tale     77

Biographies     79

# PREFACE

Trees have always fascinated my family. The first story I created at age six was about a girl who opened a door in the trunk of a fat oak and found herself in a fantasy world similar to Alice in Wonderland. My mother recorded the story but that record must have been thrown out by a well-meaning (?) family member after my parents died. I only remember the fact that a young girl was able to enter a tree and find a parallel world within it.

A painting by my mother of a gnome standing underneath a tree, holding paintbrush and palette, hung in my parents' bedroom until the mid-1980's when my father died. The painting symbolized my parents' love of woods and was a mystical connection to creativity my mother certainly felt.

In the introduction to *Their Adventurous Will*, a collection of essays about Louisiana women, I spoke of my mother as one who "gave me the ability to 'perceive tongues in trees, books in the running brooks, sermons in stone, and good in everything'*…she also gave me a love of nature…"

My father also loved the outdoors, and I wrote in one of the poems in *Let the Trees Answer*, that he often said, "Look at the trees" to pronounce a cease fire for mealtime arguments at a table overlooking three tall pines in the backyard of our home in Franklinton, Louisiana.

I can readily identify the peak months of my parents' volatile marriage as a camping trip in the woods of Hill Country Texas on the way to California during the 1940's. My mother's conversations with anyone who would listen often included references to this trip that she and my father called

---

* Act II, Scene I, *As You Like It* by William Shakespeare

"gypsying on the way to Diddy Wah Diddy."

Dr. Victoria I. Sullivan, a botanist and tree lover has spent the last forty years identifying trees and plants for me, and she joins me in this tribute to trees, photographing them in a fourth volume of a joint poetry/photography venture. I can attribute my love of nature to Vickie and my parents and appreciate their efforts to show me the consolation of spirit that plant life provides.

Diane Marquart Moore
New Iberia, Louisiana
October, 2017

# LET THE TREES ANSWER

## THE MUTENESS OF WOODED THINGS

Listening to our dark secrets at night
the hemlock practices patience,

branches reach out
wet with snow and solitude.

Beneath the scaling surface
doors open, sap rises

anxious for stories of love
to confront the darkness,

sighing for a scent of jasmine,
the sound of water flowing,

for a sudden storm
to overtake stony ground

and startle thrashers from their nests,
people from beds of complaining prayer.

Here it stands in limited space
sensing without moving,

one of the Creator's mistakes,
an angel without wings?

leaves rustling with caution,
living life in invisible time,

weeping with us at dawn
without saying a word…

## I SEE MEN, BUT THEY LOOK LIKE TREES WALKING*

Wasn't that enough
seeing trees walk,
vision restored in the blind man —
Mark's Gospel miracle?°

It was the passing of ignorance
into the embrace of trees
bearing fruit and growing,
suddenly, miraculously walking;

trunks moving about
leafless, without branches,
a forest of unrehearsed movement,
the army of truth advancing.

The blind man had sight earlier in life
lest the passage made no sense —
unbelievers would have scoffed
at this gift of restoration.

Christ wasn't aware of climate,
composition of the air, drainage,
duration of light blue
and red, irradiance —

the total environment of trees —
when he presented them
to a man suddenly partially awake
in a landscape not easy to see;

―――――――――――――

° Mark 8:22-26

majestic organisms, crowns veiled
but walking in the distance
eager to keep him hidden in woods
before they thinned out.

And where did he think they were going
in that first glimpse of blurred light
birds singing, the trees voiceless…
and seeing them walk, wasn't that enough?

## HOMECOMING

Every argument at mealtime
my father usually provoked
ended with him pounding a picnic table,
saying, "Look at the trees,"
a puzzling directive for us to cease arguing
to view pines in the backyard,
short leaf trees left behind
following a 19th century rape of longleaf pines.

My father had planted six pines,
one oak, and a mimosa
and what we saw through
the screened back porch
busy with dangling dried gourds
were pines, source of his peace
dropping fragrant needles
on our shrill voices, his violent indignities.

I never understood the power
of how a shift in viewpoint
could be effected by trees
when he threw plates of food
against the wall of peace
descending… ascending…
or the ability of trees to quiet our quarrels,
especially over spilled milk.

I could almost see
our voices splitting the scaly bark,
tree arteries absorbing family chaos,
bitter words scarring their trunks,
rings aging as we looked on
impervious to our damage
to the hearts of roots growing sluggish
by the moment.

Years later, I returned to "Look at the trees,"
three of them having plunged through
the rotting screen porch during a storm,
a town crew pushing up house

as well as the dying pines,
their death having been predicted
by their welcoming absorption…
of our mealtime arguments.

## COTTONWOOD

Somewhere near Saltillo, Mexico, close to dusk, we found lodging. It was June, and I had eaten tomatoes fresh from a Louisiana garden all the way in, washed them down with *Dos Equis* beer and wasn't hungry. The place where we stopped had a dusty courtyard that surrounded the small adobe cottage we rented. I thought I had re-entered Iran — the heat and desert-like terrain surprising me when we crossed over from Texas. Beside the cottage stood a cottonwood, my first glimpse of a tree that spoke to my travel weary condition when I heard the leather-like leaves chattering in the wind. The leaves were wider than they were long and made a pleasant sound, louder than the whispers of familiar pines growing in my yard at home.  The cottonwood, a handsome tree, was the only tree that impressed me as one that could speak in soothing tones to tired travelers. It became a favorite, and I later found abundant groves of them in California one spring when the trees began to shower their snowy blossoms. Like most objects of natural beauty, these cottonwoods were regarded as public nuisances, and I imagined them complaining among themselves about the desert dwellers' lack of appreciation for a snowstorm in June. I seldom see them in my places of residence —Louisiana and Tennessee — but I know these silver-twigged plants can talk, even sparingly, especially in Mexico where a vein of spirituality runs deep and ancient nature beliefs about the cottonwood and the afterlife have survived on *Dia de Muertos* (Day of the Dead) — when those who have died revisit earth to assure believers that all is well on the other side where cottonwoods have resettled.

## TO A CEDAR — "GERALD'S TREE[†]"

He danced around the cedar,
a pioneer species trying

---

[†] Title of painting by Georgia O'Keefe

to kill the light she sought;

"let them make pencils and incense,
this is Gerald's tree" she said.
It probably had seen 900 years.

She lit a fire and he danced,
driving away evil spirits,
offering healing for the severe figure —

a twisted tree,
red rock looming,
nothing shutting out the light

she had promised God she'd capture,
would paint the Pedernal over and over
if he made it hers,

red-blue-green horizons
land contours unlimited —
God's studio and hers.

**JOSHUA TREE**

The desert was scentless,
heat not unlike a volcano's breath,
arms of the spiky trees
uplifted in supplication
like old men grumbling to the sky
and to each other,
hostages of sunlight.

When I first saw them
spring had brought white flowers,
branches spiraling into the sky,
most of them hundreds of years old
waving welcome in a sea of sand.
They bunched together
waiting for night lizards
to scuttle in the shadows,
a squall of rain to prove
plants can't exist on sunlight alone.

A few years ago I saw their scarred arms
after a spring without rain
and a winter without frost,
deserted by orioles and wood rats
and their kind that lived thousands of years ago
threatened by climate change…
spaces in the West no longer sacred,

the Mohave gaunt from too much light,
wind blowing through skeletal trees
and fading indigo in the sky,
white-capped Joshua trees

once thriving in warm seasons of health —
the golden air of California —
destroyed.
After a long sunset,
appearing again with wider horizons,
taller stalks,
higher manifestations of life…
angular and mysterious.

## JACARANDA AFTER HURRICANE IRMA, 2017

Broken fingers of a jacaranda reach out
crying *let me in, let me in*,
the caregiver said of a tree swaying in wind,
its purple-blue flowers already gone,
desperate for the dying woman's company,
branches scraping pane for imagined comfort.

Squirrels clung to a wire fence,
swings in the park were whirling dervishes;
Hurricane Irma, an unexpected turn,
slashed the old tree's trunk
leaving white flowers of Spanish needles
untouched beside the fence.

Ancient sand ridges claimed
wounded trees outside windows
with their eyes closed,
new images formed,
fragments of memories washed
into the heart of darkness.

I was there after the air,
charged with humidity, set in again,
stifling with old jealousies and hatreds
where God had arrived by wind
scattering the tree's heart-shaped pods,
whistling at the dying woman's window:

*let me in, let me in.*

## FOR GODMOTHER DORA

*Come in April,* she said,
*when dogwoods bloom in Virginia,*
*I may die before the first blossom.*

Now He and she spring
from their graves each April —
parties of eternal return.

Twisted trees abide everywhere,
white bracts, cross shaped:
she and Christ on the hard wood,

memories of leaves
covering the face of wounds
endured too many seasons.

Trees of suffering
weighted with petals falling
into the soil of forgiveness

spreading their scarred branches
to shed the blood red berries…
of His and her rude departure.

## AMONG THE FALLEN

I wonder if the golden leaf of a maple,
moments before falling,
feels it is changing,
wind turning it inside out
this morning all in silence;

a tree announcing fall,
no life in deserted branches,
color released, bowing to death,
now a fading brown on the ground
done with its season of light.

Like the shortened life of a suicide
the leaf has disallowed time, plunging quickly,
a deliberate descent into the cool woods,
lying now in uncut grass, presuming
to know why it was cast down.

## THE SCENT OF MESQUITE

Years have passed
since I smelled the mesquite,
a sweet and clean scent
bringing memories of a dead friend,

mesquite logs blazing in the grate
competing with her cigarettes,
conversations about Charles Williams
and a copy of *Descent Into Hell*

she later gave to me.
I loved seeing her blue eyes
bright with religious inquiry
and strange prejudices.

Her family and mine picnicked together
evenings in her husband's mesquite grove
where I fried catfish, hushpuppies
in a black iron pot over a mesquite fire.

The mesquite, one of my favorite trees,
is the last to leaf out in spring
always reminds me of her
and our theological exchanges.

Twenty years passed
before I called her in Texas
to tell her how much I missed her,
the fire in the grate

and our ruminations about Williams,
his ideas about co-inherence:
the indwelling of Christ in us
and us in him… supernatural mysteries.

Her husband answered the call,
*Who in the hell is this?* he asked
and then, *She's dying.*
*Tell her I love her,* I said.

*I'll try. She's in a coma*
*Lung cancer, you know,*
*the infernal smoking.*
And he hung up.

Two days later,
I began to smell the pungent mesquite,

envisioned its branches tipped
with fern-like leaves,
yellow blossoms dropping

as if the spider-like branches
shielding Lucille had snapped
and she, like the words on Williams' headstone,
had come "under the mercy."‡.

---

‡ Engraving on headstone of Charles Williams in Holywell Cemetery, Oxford, England.

## PEARING OFF

It was green, hard and dry, apple-like in shape.
I picked one up and bit into sour flesh,
then spat it out.
The pears lay on the ground under a magnificent tree,
fruit for the picking, and I took two indoors to Grandmother
seated at the kitchen table shelling crowder peas.
"I know these were the first gift
in Twelves Days of Christmas," I said,
"but they taste like crap."
"Shush," she said, pinching my arm.

"I will wash out your mouth with Lifebuoy
even if you are nine years old and know better.
They're cooking pears. I have to open kettle them,
put them in Mason jars. It's called 'making preserves.'"
"Well, preserve me from having to eat them."

"Shush" again. "Think of the starving children in China."
"You mean those pretty, round-faced kids
who eat bowls of rice,
fresh fish, and fortune cookies?"
"I'll take a switch to you," she said.

At Thanksgiving, she served pear salad
fresh from one of her many jars,
semi-hard pears perched on a lettuce leaf,
maraschino cherry atop a dollop of mayonnaise.
"See," she said, "they're delicious."
They were thick and syrupy and tasted like crap.
"Your grandfather eats them most nights with supper."
"All I ever see him eat is cornbread in a glass of clabber."
"Shush, child, people ate this fruit in pre-historic times,
in Zurich, Switzerland and…"

"And surely we've made better food advances
after all this time. No wonder Pawpaw has peptic ulcers."
I did admire the tree's flowers,
five-petaled, snowy white blossoms appearing in spring
littering her side yard, a short-lived bower of beauty.
But I see her standing at the green-enamel stove
stirring the skinned, cut-up fruit in their own syrup,
Mason jars at attention on the sideboard of the sink,
summer labor determined to preserve
that which was hardly ever eaten.

At her death my mother and her two sisters drew straws,
no lawyer needed to divide my grandmother's earthly goods.
My mother inherited the contents of the pantry,
row after row of jars filled with what appeared to be

yellow-brown hearts swimming in mold and yeast.
"You can have these," my mother said,
"You watched her make preserves every summer."
I thought of the starving children in China,
of the beautiful tree dropping its hard fruit,
a bountiful yield for any Asian table.

"No thanks," I said. "Just take them to Good Will.
They can send them to her starving children in China.
Be sure to put her name on the label as the benefactor.
It's what she would have wanted."

## OH CHICKEN TREE, OH CHICKEN TREE

What bad press the Chinese Tallow receives:
chicken tree, popcorn tree, *boire*,
enemy of the Louisiana prairie,

noxious invader,
Yet we are startled each fall
by bright yellow, purple, and red
leaves glowing on the prairie,
an ornamental tree of dazzling beauty
offering shade to birds and lizards.

So what if its seeds hang in clusters
resembling chicken feet,
so what if the tree's sap is reputed to be poison
and it overproliferates?
The Chinese Tallow isn't selective about the soil
in which it grows or the proper drainage,
a sun lover it deplores shade,
produces the sweet nectar of honey
prized by beekeepers along the coast.

To me, the Chinese Tallow is a metaphor
for human protesters against immigrants
who have come here and produced pure stands
known as invasive species
cut down but regrowing quickly,
brilliant but condemned as disturbers
                of complacent ecosystems,
their viable seeds with popcorn faces
becoming a monoculture the protesters fear.

## WEEPING WILLOW

In my 30's I became "wispy,"
victim of a kind of Celtic melancholy
I attributed to my Scot ancestors,
felt as though I were Ophelia
falling off a willow branch
in a Shakespearean drama and drowning.

I fled to relatives in Virginia
and when my wispiness
seemed to rain the drops
resembling tears on a willow's leaf,
my Godfather combed the campus
and found a giant weeping willow.

He photographed and framed it
in a dull gray frame
as if I'd made a pact with melancholy,
would be vulnerable in the spring
when silver-tinged catkins fell
from the weeping tree.

Godmother ordered him to plant
an infant one in their side yard,
the truth being that she'd
been melancholy since birth,
thought everyone's life should be,
as she wrote: "like the sob of a cello."

In my 40's I moved the willow picture
into a shadowy hall
away from thoughts of teardrops falling,
the sun came out more often,
and Godfather sold the house
with the weeping willow in the yard.

A young couple from the Mideast
bought his house because of the tree,
unlike the former American owners
who possessed a melancholy spirit
believed that the tree with trailing leaves
symbolized for them… love and fertility.

## THE PARADISE APPLE

Were they suddenly possessed
by desire to own the tree,
eager to lose their right to joy?

And was it the crabapple
that tempted them,
a small and sour fruit

still hanging in December?
They were probably cold
in their utter nakedness

and certainly hungry
so they plucked
and ate the yellow fruit…

Each fall, the Sisters of St. Mary
harvest the wild apples,
add sugar and make delicate jelly,

telling us it is their offering
within a rhythm of hymns
and prayers to ameliorate suffering,

to lift us above the shame and guile
and our first notions of owning…
what was never ours.

## REDBUD

She bursts open
overflowing with generosity
the magenta pink
of a young girl
looking into
the mirror of spring
at her rosy face
bare stems coloring
immodestly before leafing;
a radiant body
awaiting pollination

by the long-tongued
carpenter bee
but parts of her
an old woman
ancestral bark
scaly and patchy
leaves thin and papery
and here in Appalachia
not so sacramental
her black twigs
prized by more
practical chefs
as savory seasoning
for the boiling pot
of a possum
bubbling its fat scent.

## BALD CYPRESS

Each week I pass the house,
cypress walls glinting silver in sunlight,
bald of the chaste white walls
on a neighbor's home,
its owner too cheap to paint,
replace the porch's rotting screen,

boards of aged cypress that resisted
floods and hurricanes, unremorseful,
cut from one of nature's oldest plants;
the only living thing
whose knees can be excised
and continue to thrive.

Unscented, water-loving swamp king
logged and brought to the banks
of a chastened stream
the sound of water coming near
having rushed at the tree's knees
daring to fell them,

nothing able to destroy a brazen heart,
the boards on an unpainted house
glinting silver, remembering laughter
and carrying on, new life breaking through
closed doors into dark corners, chasing away

*cauchemars*[§] hidden in the rotting screen.

---

[§] "*Cauchemars* (witches) have to count every hole in the screen before they can enter a house." *Tales From the Levee* by Marcia Gaudet

## CREPE MYRTLE

In the slow age of my brain
I could not remember her name,
the crinkled face of a long-lasting flower
everywhere in the damp air last summer,
crickets crying around her,
mottled branches wet with rain
as she shed her slippery bark,
a secret heart turned unruly.

She, desiring the immense tides of heat
in Florida parks, an icon of the South
becoming animate, as rosy as human flesh,
trembling thighs waiting for an adventurous moth
to lose its way and flutter over from India,

his loins feeding upon her dark leaves
and conceiving wild skeins of tassar silk,
a sudden engagement of seed.

## THE CATAWBA TREE

He returned home from Army duty
looking for answers in water,
deep pools he had missed
on desert maneuvers
and snow drifts of northern Maine.

When he showed me the catawba tree
I knew it was his tree,
the heart-shaped leaves,
bean pods hanging disconsolately,
a tree of melancholy demeanor

waiting for a fall wind
to stir its avowed purpose —
playing host to larvae
of sphinx moths.
How he loved their sweet smell,

the juicy catawba worm,
a yellow creature with black lines
running down its back
he plucked, bit off its head
and threw into a washtub in Pa's backyard,

hundreds of tough-skinned fish bait
telling him it was time
to do the one thing he loved,
to drop a line for fat catfish
lying on the bottom of a pond

waiting for the catawba worm.
That tree was his psyche,
its heart exposing an unrelenting angst,
home to the yellow billed cuckoo—
hope unmocked by other humans

but rapidly defoliated by the worm
feeding on leaves of a tree
I always mispronounced as the "tilapia tree,"
which  may have given real legitimacy
to it as a "fish tree."

When the worm had done its worst
stripping the leaves of a 20-foot catawba
his happiness disappeared,
something he must have felt
at one time after the catch of the day,

light fading along the edge of the pond…

## LET THE TREES ANSWER

I heard fingers snapping,
an aural moment unknown to me,
young poets expressing a kind of applause,
piercing interruptions at a poetry reading.
I heard outrage and pain in their snapping,
redress for wrongs to the black race,
ancient and in the moment.

The oaks outside captured the noise
and held it inside skeins of moss,
wanting to tell those gathered
that patience… loving kindness… endurance
are as old as rage and injustice
and they had witnessed all,
their gnarled bark testament
to the suffering beneath.

They were dropping acorns,
no turning back for them,
a snapping sound of their own
as the nuts rained down
the sound of restoration and rebirth,
the sound of nothing is ever lost,
lordly oaks trying to say:
the cost of being human is suffering —
white, black, yellow, mixed—
            no skin exempt, even in its grandeur.

# EVERYDAY JOURNAL II.

## SHOE POLISH PHILOSOPHY

On a cold day in the silence
of too much winter,
ambitious only for the scent
of Kiwi polish and shoe leather,
I polished shoes
thinking of my father
building this crude shoeshine box,
the wooden form of a large foot
for the one pair of shoes
he bought us every year.

Cordovan, black, brown paste,
skinned toes of worn shoes —
we lived between the scuff and the shine,
smelled the healing wax
that nourishes scarred leather,
each time color returning more deeply
when buffed hard to gloss.
No excuse to buy new ones often —
paste wax, flannel cloth, black bristled brush —
up to us to put our best foot forward.

# SYNCHRONICITY

It happens all the time.
I dream about a subject.
A related incident occurs.
Book titles appear underhand.
Similar internet subjects pop up.
The telephone rings
and a caller echoes my thoughts.
TV stories reveal my subject.
These messages from the universe
I can only conclude
are meant for me to dedicate
a poem, a sermon, a novel,
an individual event translated
to a universal message,
provocation to share
a crone's wisdom
while a crow outside my window
perched in a dead tree
mocks my unsettling stories.

## THE NEWSPAPERS FORETOLD

a death in each tubular
plastic bound edition,
fourteen at last count
removed by a caring neighbor
and placed at the back door.

She missed the day it happened,
red lights flashing,
caretakers scurrying outside.
Death in all its calamities
now staring at us in the daily newspaper

rolled up tight, a rubber band around,
the all-night, beaming garage light,
for months Illuminating eerie emptiness,
turned off at last,
wondering who's next.

The silent motor launch,
"T-Bag" carved above the prow
redolent with smell of crab
and its windshield still muddy,
beached behind the fence.

## INNER SANCTUM

About four doors down
same side of street as the lately dead,
one side of garage doors
suddenly opens,
exposing agoraphobic illusions.

Through a wide crack
we see assorted boxes, clothing,
discarded pots, pans
overflowing from headquarters,
the detritus of a hoarder

spilling into the street.
Four weeks later, still culling,
a relative parks a black car
in the frozen drive
blocking our view;

worldly goods exhumed,
gate on the wooden fence
hanging by one board;
all her fears scattered
about our quiet street.

Who will be next
in the bright cold,
January's winter hex?
Will our hands never get warm
In central heat's invisible flames?

One man's warm hands take blankets
to homeless forms huddled under bridges
oblivious to the Interstate vibrating overhead,
makes soup for those yet alive,
unafraid of the world out there.

## REPTILIAN COLD

Green trees recede to tan
and iguanas fall from them,
lie immobile beneath.
Pythons perish in the Everglades
where they have known languor
and warmth and greenness.
And when, we ask,
will the season go south again,
recapture the sky of good weather?
When will the iguanas,
like smaller forms of Lazarus,
rise in the sunlight
to flick their tails
at those cold shoulders
the ravaged trees have turned to them?

# WATCHING A MOVIE ABOUT VAN GOGH

Rain falls on dead ginger leaves
scattered beside the broken fence,
two patches of brown folded inward,
light surging away
in the melancholy of devil's snow.

They called Van Gogh "melancholic,"
thought his inner darkness evil;
after all, the sun beamed on his red beard,
a half-hearted moon on his horizon.
He lived a life of shadowy incaution.

No one knew then why the sky within
was not something he made purposefully,
they only knew a blue sky, a yellow sun
as colors they could come back to each day,
and he seldom felt where they had been.

Melancholic meant sad without cause,
feelings they could not,
would not share with him.
Compassion was not their true art,
that was the way of *Auvers-sur-Oise*.

No one knows if he shot himself
that close to having left the asylum
or if he was victimized by young men taunting,
stealing his easel and paints,
sending him to the cheerless bed

where a doctor sobbed over his failure
to cure Genius of enviable art,
space and time no longer mattering
to the body lying curled around a dream…
a field of big-faced sunflowers.

## II.

Here, the sunflowers are rivaled
by first blooms of camellia
flooding out winter,
melancholy reversed,
a transfiguration of faces.
Crows caw noisily
trying to annihilate the sense of things
in a hybrid flower
making the world pink with light
over its yellow center.

I am sorry Van Gogh never saw those blooms
nor heard their voices
reading poems in the shadowy house,
following the sun past curtains
into the doorway of the coulee.
A tall bush staring at plunging bees
at the edge of water
near curled ginger that asks for little,
and dead aloe far from the desert,
gracious blooms in the withering air.

# EMERGENCE

A peahen landed in the backyard,
air bubbling with the end of ice,
south winds blowing away mist.

The bejeweled creature, refusing to show her tail,
passed closed doors along the coulee
looking for a mate or food;

a brief glimpse of iridescent green
she stopped short of the neighbor's fence,
boards rotting from too much winter,

then lifted off before we knew
whether it was spring arriving…
or winter departing.

# CARDINAL TALE

Two cardinals trespassed on the patio
pecking at red concrete, suspended hopes,
a frivolous landing, brown and red flashing
at the smeared pane of false spring.

They seemed puzzled by sudden bursts of azaleas
St. Francis feeding birds in one corner,
and I see them as my transformed parents,
mother and father gently rupturing a calm morning

without loud cries of disagreement
or shattered glass,
a brief vividness soon on wing,
the sun, a possibility foretelling

joy hidden among curled leaves,
intrepid cardinals come to tell me
I am on the margins of another life
banked in the space of no time…

## AUTHOR

Diane Marquart Moore is a poet, journalist, book author, and blogger at *A Word's Worth*, who divides her time between Sewanee, Tennessee and New Iberia, Louisiana. She is a regular contributor to the *Pinyon Review*, has published in *The Southwestern Review* at the University of Louisiana, Lafayette, Louisiana, *Interdisciplinary Humanities*, *The Xavier Review*, *Acadiana Profile Magazine*, *American Weave*, *Louisiana Historical Review*, *Trace*, and other literary journals. She has been an Associate Editor for *Acadiana Lifestyle Magazine*, New Iberia, Louisiana, feature writer and columnist for *The Daily Iberian*, New Iberia, Louisiana, as well as a feature writer and book reviewer for *The Yaddasht Haftegy* in Ahwaz, Iran where she lived during the reign of the Shahanshah. Her young adult book, *Martin's Quest*, was a finalist in the Heekins Foundation Award Contest and was selected to be on the supplementary reading list for gifted and talented students by the Louisiana Library Association. Moore is also a retired archdeacon of the Episcopal Diocese of Western Louisiana.

## PHOTOGRAPHER

Victoria I. Sullivan is a writer, botanist, and photographer. She studied biology at the University of Miami, earned a Ph.D. in biology from Florida State University and held a faculty position in the Department of Biology at the University of Louisiana, Lafayette for 20 years. She has published poetry, flash fiction, many botanical papers and other nonfiction, and two speculative fiction sequels, *Adoption* and *Rogue Genes*, and a book for nature enthusiasts, *Why Water Plants Don't Drown*. Sullivan is a resident of Sewanee, Tennessee, and winters in New Iberia, Louisiana.

www.ingramcontent.com/pod-product-compliance
Lightning Source LLC
Chambersburg PA
CBHW042326150426
43193CB00001B/7